OUTDOOR PHOTOGRAPHY

By John Hamilton

Abdo & Daughters
An imprint of Abdo Publishing | abdopublishing.com

abdopublishing.com

Published by Abdo Publishing, a division of ABDO, PO Box 398166, Minneapolis, Minnesota 55439. Copyright © 2019 by Abdo Consulting Group, Inc. International copyrights reserved in all countries. No part of this book may be reproduced in any form without written permission from the publisher. Abdo & Daughters™ is a trademark and logo of Abdo Publishing.

Printed in the United States of America, North Mankato, Minnesota.
052018
092018

THIS BOOK CONTAINS
RECYCLED MATERIALS

Editor: Sue Hamilton
Copy Editor: Bridget O'Brien
Graphic Design: Sue Hamilton
Cover Design: Candice Keimig and Pakou Moua
Cover Photos: John Hamilton
Interior Images: Eastman-Kodak-pg 6 (top); Fujifilm North America-pg 11; Getty-pg 30; iStock-pgs 6 (bottom), 9 (top), 10, 15 (bottom), 16 (top), 18 (top), 19 (bottom), 20, 21 (top), 32, 34 (bottom), 38, 39, 40-41, 44 & 45 (top); John Hamilton-pgs 4-5, 12, 13, 14, 15 (top), 16 (bottom), 17, 19 (top), 22, 23, 24-25, 26, 27, 28, 29, 31, 33, 34 (top), 35, 36, 37, 42 & 43; Nikon USA-pg 7 (inset), 8, 12 (inset), 13 (inset), 14 (inset), 15 (inset) & 18 (bottom); Shutterstock-pgs 7, 9 (bottom) & 21 (bottom); U.S. Copyright Office-pg 45 (bottom).

Library of Congress Control Number: 2017963907
Publisher's Cataloging-in-Publication Data
Names: Hamilton, John, author.
Title: Outdoor photography / by John Hamilton.
Description: Minneapolis, Minnesota : Abdo Publishing, 2019. | Series: Digital photography | Includes online resources and index.
Identifiers: ISBN 9781532115875 (lib.bdg.) | ISBN 9781532156809 (ebook)
Subjects: LCSH: Outdoor photography--Juvenile literature. | Nature photography--Juvenile literature. | Nature in art--Juvenile literature. | Photography--Digital techniques--Juvenile literature.
Classification: DDC 778.71--dc23

CONTENTS

THE CALL OF THE WILD

Nature photographers face unique challenges. Like all photographers, they must balance proper exposure, focus, and camera angles. But they also often use specialized field equipment, such as lightweight yet sturdy tripods, telephoto lenses, and filters.

Most importantly, there is nature itself. The weather can be fickle, and hiking to remote locations is often challenging. But the rewards are great. Not only do outdoor photographers come home with stunning images, they get to be out in the wild, enjoying some of the best scenery Mother Earth has to offer.

HOW TO CREATE DEPTH AND SCALE

Try putting an object of known size in the frame. In this case, the object is a photographer along the Bright Angel Trail, in Arizona's Grand Canyon National Park. Hold this book at arm's length and cover the man up with your thumb. The photo becomes flat and not as interesting. As a foreground object of a known size, he adds depth and scale, tricking the brain into thinking this is a three-dimensional scene.

CAMERAS

Digital photography captures a scene when light passes through a lens and is focused onto an image sensor. The sensor converts the light into digital form. It is then stored as a file that can be transferred to a computer for later processing, or even shared immediately on social media. The first portable digital camera was made by Eastman Kodak in 1975. It weighed 8 pounds (3.6 kg) and shot only in black-and-white. Digital cameras as we know them today first became popular in the 1990s and early 2000s.

The first portable digital camera was made by Steven Sasson for Eastman Kodak in 1975.

Before digital photography, images were captured on film. Most photographers today have long given up film because of the big advantages of digital. One of the best parts is seeing your photos right away so you can change settings if needed. Another advantage is the large number of shots you can take.

Many modern digital cameras are lightweight and easy to carry.

With a DSLR (Digital Single Lens Reflex) camera, you can look through the viewfinder or use the camera's screen display to see exactly what you're shooting.

Most professional landscape photographers today use DSLR (Digital Single Lens Reflex) cameras. With a DSLR, you actually peer through the camera lens so you can see exactly what you're shooting. Angle of view and sharpness are determined by the lens. DSLR lenses are "interchangeable," which means you can change one lens for another depending on your creative needs.

Once light travels inside the DSLR, it is diverted by a mirror into a glass prism, which directs the light into the viewfinder. When you press the shutter release button, the "reflex" mirror flips up and the shutter behind it opens. Light strikes the image processor. After the exposure, the shutter closes, and the mirror flips back down.

The image sensor inside the camera has millions of light-capturing pixels that record an image. The greater the number of pixels, the higher the resolution of the picture. A 20-megapixel (20-million-pixel) sensor almost

The inside workings of a DSLR camera.

always has a better resolution than a 10-megapixel sensor. Modern DSLR sensors usually come equipped with at least 16 to 24 megapixels. Some have 40 megapixels or more. However, the number of pixels on an image sensor is only one part of a picture's quality. The size of the image sensor is also important. The bigger the better, usually. The large sensors in many DSLRs produce the most detailed pictures. That is an advantage when capturing grand landscapes.

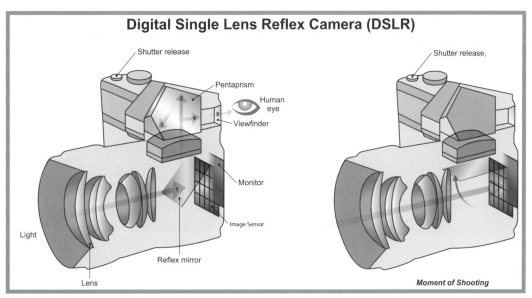

Digital Single Lens Reflex Camera (DSLR)

Shutter release

Pentaprism

Human eye

Viewfinder

Monitor

Light

Image Sensor

Reflex mirror

Lens

Shutter release,

Moment of Shooting

This diagram shows how a DSLR camera creates a photograph.

8 TIPS **FOR CARING FOR YOUR** CAMERA

1. Use an air blower and microfiber cloth to clean your camera regularly.
2. Use a strap when carrying your camera.
3. When not in use, keep the camera safe in a bag or case.
4. Many photographers put a UV or skylight filter on the front of their lenses. These block ultraviolet rays from the Sun (which degrade image quality) and protect your expensive lenses from dust or scratches.
5. Make sure you always have spare batteries.
6. Keep your camera out of the rain.
7. Keep your camera out of hot cars.
8. Never leave your camera unattended.

Cell phones are commonly used as both a primary and a backup camera. Most cell phones have a complicated lens arrangement. This has helped improve their photo quality greatly in recent years.

There is an old saying that the best camera is the one you have on you. For many people, that means a cell phone. The image quality of most cell phones has greatly improved in recent years. Most professional photographers carry one as a backup in case their DSLRs are not handy when a photo opportunity arises. Cell phones do the focusing and adjust exposure for you. You can also use apps that give you more control. There are clip-on lenses that allow you to shoot wide-angle or telephoto photos.

Cell phone cameras do have disadvantages. It usually takes longer to set up a shot than with a DSLR. Adjusting exposure with an app and attaching a clip-on lens can be awkward. In addition, cell phone cameras are tricky in low-light situations. Be sure to hold it steady, or even use a tripod with a special mount, to avoid blurry photos.

Mirrorless cameras are becoming more popular each year. Like DSLRs, different lenses can be mounted on most of them (some have fixed lenses). However, there is no mirror or glass prism. This makes mirrorless cameras lightweight and quiet to shoot. Yet, they have excellent image quality, even in low light.

If you are a beginner, don't worry too much about which camera to buy. Think about what you want to do with it and which features are important to you. Amazing images can be taken with almost all digital cameras sold today. Their quality gets better each year. The truth is, it's the eye (and the mind) behind the camera that matters most. Creative photographers can make world-class images no matter what they're shooting with.

A mirrorless camera produced by Fujifilm. This type of camera is lightweight and quiet to shoot, yet produces excellent image quality, even in low light.

LENSES

Just as important as your camera are the lenses you use. They determine the "field of view" of your scene. A wide-angle lens shows more of the surrounding area. A telephoto captures just a small part, which is why everything looks magnified.

A lens's field of view is measured in millimeters. A "normal" field of view captured by a full-frame image sensor is about 50mm. That is about the same as what you perceive with your eyes. Common wide-angle lenses are about 24mm to 35mm. Super-wide lenses start at about 10mm. Below that are fisheye lenses, which are used for special effects because of their distortion.

The photo shows the distortion that occurs with a fisheye lens.

A wide-angle lens captures much of the surrounding area.

Most landscape photographers own at least one wide-angle lens. (Wide-angle zooms are a popular choice.) These lenses make it possible to capture vast scenic vistas. They work well in low light. They also have a tremendous range of focus, or "depth of field." That makes it easy to keep everything in your scene in sharp focus, from a foreground flower to a background mountain.

FILTERS

There are two "must have" filters for outdoor photographers. Filters are screwed onto the front of the lens, or inserted into a special holder. Polarizer filters cut down on reflections and darken blue skies for a dramatic effect. Graduated neutral density filters are dark on top and become clear on the bottom. They help balance the exposure between a dark ground and a light sky.

EXPOSURE

A camera's shutter-speed dial.

Exposure is the amount of light that strikes the camera's image sensor. The "correct" exposure for a scene depends on three settings. They include ISO, shutter speed, and aperture. All three work together.

ISO is the image sensor's sensitivity to light. If you start with an ISO of 100 and increase it to 200, you make the sensor twice as sensitive. However, the higher the ISO, the more digital noise is created. The lower the ISO, the better the quality. For example, when shooting in bright sunlight, you would normally set a low ISO. However, in dim scenes, you might increase the ISO. Otherwise, your exposures would be so long that you couldn't hold your camera steady, or your subject's movements would cause blurring.

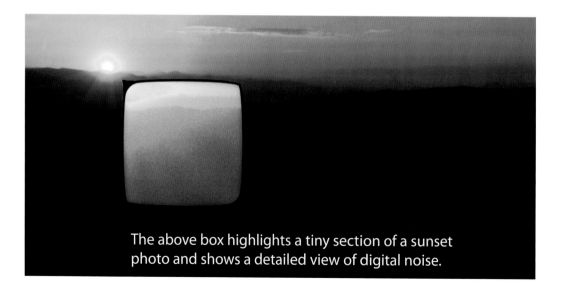

The above box highlights a tiny section of a sunset photo and shows a detailed view of digital noise.

Choosing the right exposure for a landscape scene is a balance between areas of light and dark (tone) and focus (depth of field). These are controlled by the right combination of ISO, shutter speed, and aperture.

Shutter speed is the length of time the shutter opens to let light strike the image sensor. It is measured in seconds (usually a fraction of a second). Each setting is twice as long, or half as short, as the setting next to it. For example, 1/250 second is twice as fast as the next setting, 1/125 second. Shutter speeds must be fairly fast to avoid blur from camera shake, usually in the range of 1/125 to 1/250 second. Wide-angle lenses can be used with slower shutter speeds.

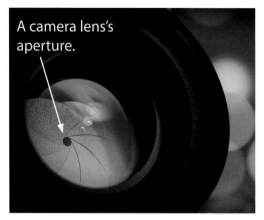
A camera lens's aperture.

Lenses have apertures, or holes, in the back where they are mounted to the camera. Apertures can be adjusted much like the irises in your eyes. They are measured in "f-stops." The *smaller* the f-stop number, the *more* light is allowed into the camera.

The important thing to remember is that if you increase one setting, such as shutter speed, then you must reduce the other setting (aperture) in order to get back to your original exposure.

When you are starting out, it's okay to put your camera on automatic. DSLRs have a setting on the exposure dial called "P," which stands for program mode. Modern cameras are like small computers. They examine the scene and figure out the math for you. The camera will pick a shutter speed and aperture combination. That will allow you to concentrate on other things, like focus and composition.

The exposure dial is set at "P" for program mode.

18

The small, or "shallow," depth of field in this photo ensures that only the aspen trees are sharp, which brings attention to the subject.

As you get more practice taking pictures, you'll soon want to control these settings yourself in creative ways. For example, controlling the aperture also controls the amount of depth of field in your scene. That means you have control over what is in sharp focus.

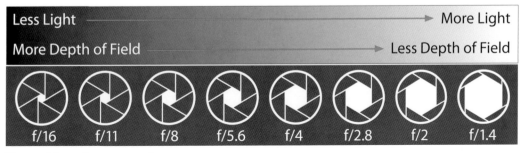

Typical lens f-stop settings.

GETTING A STEADY SHOT

If there's one piece of equipment every outdoor photographer should own, it's a sturdy tripod. A lot of landscape shooting happens at dawn or dusk, when light levels are low. You simply cannot handhold your camera and expect sharp results, especially with telephoto lens. You can raise your camera's ISO to make it more sensitive to light, but that reduces quality by increasing digital noise. For rock-steady photos with the best quality, get a tripod.

Tripods come in many shapes and sizes, and some can be quite expensive. In general, the better tripods are heavy (to give your camera a solid platform), made of metal or carbon fiber, and have adjustable-length tubular legs. If you are backpacking in the wilderness, you might not want to lug around heavy gear. You can certainly buy a tripod that is lighter, but remember that your images may not be as sharp.

What if you come across a once-in-a-lifetime scene and don't happen to have your tripod nearby? Don't despair! There are things you can do to give yourself a better chance of capturing a sharp image. Hold your camera with your elbows tucked in near your body. The camera should rest in the palm of your hand. Also, look for objects around you to rest your camera against, like a big rock or even the trunk of a sturdy tree.

BEST **SHUTTER** SPEED

If you're handholding your camera, how do you know if the shutter speed is fast enough to create a sharp image? The rule of thumb is to shoot at a shutter speed higher than the reciprocal of the focal length of your lens. In other words, if you're shooting with a 200mm lens, you'll need a shutter speed of at least 1/200 second in order to get a sharp picture. If you're shooting with a wide-angle 24mm lens, you can go all the way down to 1/24 second. If you set your camera to "Program" or "Auto," it will calculate this for you.

COMPOSITION

Composition is where the creative photographer gets a chance to shine. You don't need fancy equipment or exotic locations to make a stunning image. Composition is all about arranging the scene in your viewfinder in the best way to tell your story.

Good composition uses many artistic elements. That includes the use of color, contrast, texture, framing, and natural lines. All of these elements lead the viewer's eye to your subject. One of the most important things is to reduce clutter in your scene, and the best way to do that is to fill the frame with your subject. Be aware of empty space around your subject and get closer if you can.

Some of the most striking landscape photos have a strong foreground element, such as large rocks, flowers, or a beach in front of a lake. Foreground elements create a feeling of depth. It is an illusion that makes the viewer feel like stepping into your scene. It is certainly not the only way to shoot a landscape, but it's very popular today. You have to find the right style that fits your vision.

THE RULE OF THIRDS

The "rule of thirds" is a way of dividing the viewfinder into sections and arranging your subject within the lines. Instead of a "rule," think of it as a helpful guideline. Divide your viewfinder into three horizontal parts, and three vertical parts. Put your subject roughly near one of the intersecting lines. Don't always place your horizons in the center of the frame. If you want to emphasize a great sky, put your horizon in the lower third. If you're more interested in the ground, the horizon goes in the upper third.

QUALITY OF LIGHT

There are two times of day that are the best for shooting outdoor photos: dawn and dusk. For roughly 30 minutes before and after the Sun rises or sets, the quality of light becomes warm and soft. Shadows become softer. Everything seems to glow. Landscape photographers call this the "magic hour" or "golden hour." Those striking images you see in magazines or on the web? Nine out of 10 times, they were shot during the golden hour. Of course, this means you'll have to rise early, or skip dinner, to capture those magnificent sunrises and sunsets. It is well worth the effort.

An end-of-the-day rainstorm produced a beautiful rainbow over a dramatic landscape near Moab, Utah. Dusk and dawn are the two best times of day for outdoor photography. The roughly 30 minutes before and after the Sun rises or sets is known as the "magic hour" or "golden hour."

BAD WEATHER

When bad weather strikes, many photographers pack their gear and head home. Stick around! Some of the best light happens during these times. Right after a storm, shafts of light might strike a mountain, framed by dark clouds on the horizon. Fog and mist create very dramatic landscapes. Or if you're really lucky, a desert rainbow might appear, like the above scene after a thunderstorm in Utah's Dead Horse State Park. If lightning is anywhere in the vicinity, *take cover immediately*. Your tripod makes a great lightning rod!

MOTION

One of the coolest parts of photography is being able to freeze action. When something is moving so fast that the eye can barely perceive it, the camera can capture one split second of its motion. The results can be breathtaking. The other side of the coin is to purposely create blur to give the illusion of motion.

Both of these camera effects are created by controlling your shutter speed. To stop the action of a speeding horse, track star, or bird of prey, you'll want a shutter speed of 1/500 second or faster. Some DSLR cameras can reach shutter speeds of 1/4,000 second. To balance your exposure, sunny days are best. You might even have to increase your ISO to at least 400 or higher.

This rodeo scene was frozen using a shutter speed of 1/2,000 second, with an f-stop of f/2.8 and ISO 640.

The Middle Falls at Gooseberry Falls State Park in northern Minnesota. The silky water effect came from a shutter speed of 1/5 second, with an f-stop of f/16 and ISO 100.

To create blur in a moving subject, slow your shutter speed down to 1/15 second or slower. Waterfalls and rivers look more realistic when you create motion blur. The longer the exposure, the silkier the water looks. You'll definitely want to shoot on a tripod to make sure the rest of the scene stays sharp.

SUNRISES AND SUNSETS

Sunrises and sunsets are some of the most crowd-pleasing photos you can take. People just seem to like them. They can also be difficult to shoot when the bright light overwhelms your camera's sensor. The built-in light meter sees all that brightness and overcompensates with a fast shutter speed and a small aperture. That gives you a darkened photo that isn't anywhere near as majestic as the scene you tried to capture.

A hazy sunset at North Dakota's Theodore Roosevelt National Park is enhanced with a graduated orange filter.

Here's a trick to shooting better sunsets and sunrises: point your camera at the sky above, without the Sun showing in the viewfinder. Hold your shutter button halfway down. That locks the exposure. While still holding the button halfway down, recompose the image the way you want it, then take the picture. That should give you deep colors and enough exposure in the foreground to make the scene interesting and beautiful, just the way you remember it. (You might need to focus manually before setting your exposure.)

For several minutes after sunset, the sky is a deep blue, and clouds can change to beautiful shades of red, orange, and purple. If you're out hiking, bring a flashlight so you can make your way safely back to camp!

Wind turbines spin in a field in northern Iowa. No color filters were used; that is the natural color a few minutes after sunset. The turbine blades were given a slight motion blur by using a shutter speed of 1/8 second.

BLACK-AND-WHITE LANDSCAPES

There is a long tradition of shooting landscapes in black-and-white (monochrome). Stripped of color, these images are about pure form. Textures seem to pop off the page. In the hands of a skilled black-and-white landscape photographer, a scene can become a work of art.

One of the greatest black-and-white landscape photographers in the world was Ansel Adams (1902-1984). His work was simple, pure, and elevated nature to something sacred. He shot his most

Ansel Adams

famous images on film with large-format cameras, which he lugged through the wilderness. Today, with smaller digital cameras, we can model our own images after Adams's photography. Color photos are easily converted to black-and-white in the digital darkroom. From there, we are limited only by our own artistic vision and lessons learned from the old masters.

"Thunderstorm at Twin Lakes" by John Hamilton.

ANIMALS

The most important skill to have when photographing animals is patience. Wild animals have their own timetable, and it doesn't include you. They won't pose or look your way when you tell them to. You have to be ready with your camera and wait for the right moment. You might have to wait hours—or even days—to get that award-winning shot. All that waiting can be its own reward. You learn about the animals you're trying to photograph, their habits, when they appear in the open, and when they retreat to the woods. And once you learn about the animals, it becomes easier to anticipate the right moment to capture them with your camera.

A wildlife photographer keeps his distance, but still gets the shot.

A wild mountain goat sharing a hiking path in Montana's Glacier National Park.

The feathery details of a Florida heron are captured with a 210mm lens.

Professional wildlife photographers have very specialized—and expensive—equipment. That includes long, heavy telephoto lenses. You don't need pro gear when you're starting out. An 80-200mm zoom lens might be all you need at first.

Here's a trick: Many DSLRs today take pictures with such a high number of pixels that you can later crop quite close to the subject and still get a perfectly good final result. That's a lot less expensive than buying a super-telephoto lens.

Tripods can help steady your shots, but they are often cumbersome as you move through the wilderness. A good compromise is a monopod. It attaches to your camera like a tripod, but has just one leg. It is often steady enough to get a good shot, yet it is lightweight and portable.

A monopod is a lightweight alternative to a heavy tripod.

A grizzly bear mom and cubs are photographed from the safety of a car in Yellowstone National Park.

When trying to get close to wildlife, you may want to wear camouflage clothing. Rest assured, however, the animals know you're there. It's best simply to approach slowly and let them get used to your presence. You can tell if they start to get nervous. They may bolt just when you think you can get a good shot. Stick with your subjects and wait to see what they'll do. Be patient, and learn how close you can get. (But don't get too close. Treat wild animals with respect. They can be dangerous when threatened, and besides, you're the one invading their homes.)

A golden-mantled ground squirrel in Colorado's Rocky Mountain National Park.

Use your telephoto lens for wildlife close-ups. When you want to show animals in their native habitat, use a wider lens. It's always interesting to show animals interacting with their surroundings.

To get really interesting wildlife photos, try to get down to the same level as the animals. That often means getting on your belly. This also works well for photographing pets.

Get to the same level as your subject for great pet photos.

You don't have to go far to photograph wildlife. Great shots can be found right in your own backyard. If you're patient, you may be surprised to

A chance sighting of an eagle eating its lunch on the roof of a house made for a fascinating photo.

encounter animals such as deer, coyotes, wild turkeys, hawks, bald eagles, rabbits, and many other interesting creatures.

ZOOS

When photographing animals in zoos, patience is the key. Your subjects might not always be in the best position. Try to frame them in a way that avoids showing fences or other artificial structures (unless that is your intent, of course). Use your zoom lens to crop in close, or use a wide-angle lens to show how the animals live in their artificial world.

Gibbon,
Henry Doorly Zoo
Omaha, Nebraska

SPECIAL SITUATIONS

WINTER

The most important thing to know about shooting outside in winter is that white snow will trick your camera's light meter. The scene will be underexposed, making the snow appear dull gray. Correct this by slightly overexposing, turning the snow white again. DSLRs have an exposure value (EV) setting for overriding the camera. Set it to overexpose by about +1, or even +2. Take a few test pictures and check them. Adjust the EV setting if necessary.

Modern cameras are powered by batteries, which drain quickly in the cold. Keep spares warm in your pocket until they're needed.

California's Yosemite National Park.

CHRISTMAS LIGHTS

Getting good shots of Christmas lights is all about timing. If you start shooting when there's too much light in the sky, the Christmas lights will barely show up. If you wait until it's completely dark, you'll only capture the lights themselves. The rest of the scene will be mostly black.

Start shooting shortly after sunset, when you can still see detail in your surroundings. You want the sky to be about the same brightness as the Christmas lights. Use a tripod, and set your shutter speed to about 1/4 second. You might eventually go up to a full second. Start shooting, and check the images on the screen in back of your camera. Adjust the exposure as needed. You'll have about a 10- to 15-minute window to catch that magical shot where the colorful Christmas lights balance beautifully with a deep blue sky.

FIREWORKS

For fireworks, set your camera to its lowest ISO setting for the best quality, and then put it on a tripod. You'll be using very slow shutter speeds to capture the light trails of the explosions. Use a medium telephoto lens, such as 200mm, if you want to capture the fireworks fully in your frame. Otherwise, zoom out to about 24mm or 28mm to capture the surroundings.

You'll be shooting in manual mode. Set your shutter speed to about 4 seconds, with an aperture of f/11 or f/8.

Take a test shot and check it out on the LCD screen on the back of your camera. If it's too bright, lower the exposure to 2 or 3 seconds. Keep testing until you get the results you want. When the fireworks display really gets going, you'll get several explosions during that multi-second exposure.

THE DIGITAL DARKROOM

Photos taken with modern cameras are usually well exposed and in focus, but there's always room for improvement. That's where the digital darkroom comes in. Fixing a photo's range of tones (its light and dark pixels) can improve it dramatically. Color balance, sharpening, and cropping are also common enhancements. These are all easy to perform on modern digital photo software, such as Photoshop, Lightroom, or GIMP. There are even inexpensive apps for cell phones that let you experiment with your photos.

Image editing software can be difficult to learn, but it is a fun way to improve your photos. Use the software's help menus, or search for online video instructions. Everyone was a beginner once, and many generous photographers are happy to share their skills.

Postproduction work can dramatically enhance a photo.

A lone hiker surveys the desert canyons in Utah's Dead Horse State Park. The photo above is before image enhancement. In Photoshop, the first task was to fix the tonal range with a "levels" adjustment. That took care of the flat light in the scene. Color vibrance was boosted to enhance the red rocks. Some dodging was applied to make the foreground rocks and the hiker stand out better.

INDEX